When the Dark Comes Dancing

A BEDTIME POETRY BOOK

compiled by Nancy Larrick

illustrated by John Wallner

PHILOMEL BOOKS
NEW YORK

First published in 1983 by Philomel Books,
a division of The Putnam Publishing Group,
51 Madison Avenue, New York, N.Y. 10010.
Text copyright © 1983 by Nancy Larrick
Illustrations copyright © 1983 by John Wallner
All rights reserved. Printed in the United States of America.

Library of Congress Cataloging in Publication Data
Main entry under title: When the dark comes dancing.
Bibliography: p. 73. Includes index.
SUMMARY: A collection of poems, lullabies, and lyrics
especially chosen to be read at bedtime.
1. Children's poetry. 2. Lullabies. 1. Poetry—
Collections. 2. Night—Poetry I. Larrick, Nancy.
II. Wallner, John C. III. Title: Bedtime poetry book.
PN6109.97.W48 808.81 81-428
ISBN 0-399-20807-0 AACR1

Second Impression

Copyright Acknowledgments

The editor and Philomel Books would like to thank the following for permission to reprint the selections in this book. All possible care has been taken to trace the ownership of every selection included and to make full acknowledgment for its use. If any errors have accidentally occurred, they will be corrected in subsequent editions, provided notification is sent to the publishers:
by Ivy O. Eastwick, copyright © 1960, Abingdon Press. Reprinted by permission of Abingdon Press.

Addison-Wesley Publishing Company, Inc., for "Little Donkey Close Your Eyes," from *Nibble, Nibble* by Margaret Wise Brown, copyright © 1959, Margaret Wise Brown. Reprinted by permission of Addison-Wesley Publishing Company, Inc.

Angus & Robertson Publishers, Australia, for "The Train in the Night," from *Traveller's Joy* by Elizabeth Riddell, copyright © 1961, Elizabeth Riddell. Reprinted by permission of the author and Angus & Robertson Publishers, Sydney, Australia.

Blackie and Son Limited, for "Benue Lullaby," from *Poems For Africa* by Martin Brennan. Reprinted by permission of Blackie and Son Limited.

Basil Blackwell Publisher, for "Last Song," by James Guthrie, from *Time for Poetry* by Arbuthnot and Root. Reprinted by permission of Basil Blackwell Publisher.

Cambridge University Press, for "An African Lullaby," from *African Poetry*, edited by Ulli Beier. Reprinted by permission of Cambridge University Press.

William Collins Sons and Company, Ltd., for "Hushabye My Darling" and "All Tucked in and Roasty Toasty," from *Catch Me & Kiss Me & Say It Again* by Clyde and Wendy Watson, copyright © 1978, Clyde Watson. Reprinted by permission of William Collins Sons and Company, Ltd., London.

Thomas Y. Crowell, Publishers, and Macmillan, London and Basingstoke, for "Rock, rock, sleep my baby," from *Father Fox's Pennyrhymes* by Clyde Watson, copyright © 1971, Clyde Watson. Reprinted by permission of Thomas Y. Crowell, Publishers, and Macmillan, London and Basingstoke.

Thomas Y. Crowell, Publishers, for "Dreams," from *In One Door and Out the Other* by Aileen Fisher, copyright © 1969, Aileen Fisher. Reprinted by permission of Thomas Y. Crowell, Publishers.

Curtis Brown, Ltd., for "Hush 'n' Bye," from *American Folk Songs for Children* by Ruth Crawford Seeger, copyright © 1948, Ruth Crawford Seeger, copyright renewed 1976, Michael Seeger. Reprinted by permission of Curtis Brown, Ltd.

Doubleday & Company, Inc., for "Sleep, Baby, Sleep," from *Favorite Poems Old and New*, edited by Helen Ferris, copyright © 1957, Helen Ferris Tibbets; for "Hush, Little Baby," from *The Great Songbook*, edited by Timothy John, copyright © 1978, Ernest Benn Limited, published by Doubleday & Company, Inc. in the United States. Reprinted by permission of Doubleday and Company, Inc.

E. P. Dutton & Company, Inc., for "Sleeping Outdoors" and "Winter Night," from *Rhymes About Us* by Marchette Chute, copyright © 1974, Marchette Chute. Reprinted by permission of E. P. Dutton & Company, Inc.

Aileen Fisher, for "Until We Built a Cabin," from *That's Why* by Aileen Fisher, copyright © 1946, Aileen Fisher, copyright renewed 1974, Aileen Fisher, published by Thomas Nelson and Sons, New York. Reprinted by permission of the author.

Douglas Gibson, for "Cat in Moonlight," from *Happy Landings*, compiled by Howard Sergeant, originally published by Evans Brothers Ltd., London, 1971. Now published by Bell & Hyman Limited, London. Reprinted by permission of Douglas Gibson.

Grosset & Dunlap, Inc., for "Storm at Night," from *The Sparrow Bush* by Elizabeth Coatsworth, copyright © 1966, Grosset & Dunlap, Inc., Reprinted by permission of Grosset & Dunlap, Inc.

Harcourt Brace Jovanovich, Inc., for "Dream," from *Wide Awake and Other Poems* by Myra Cohn Livingston, copyright © 1959, Myra Cohn Livingston; and "My Star," from *The Moon and A Star and Other Poems* by Myra Cohn Livingston, copyright © 1965, Myra Cohn Livingston. Reprinted by permission of Harcourt Brace Jovanovich, Inc.

Harper & Row, Publishers, Inc., for "The Middle of the Night," from *In the Middle of the Trees* by Karla Kuskin, copyright © 1958, Karla Kuskin. Reprinted by permission of Harper & Row, Publishers, Inc.

Harper & Row, Publishers, Inc. and The Bodley Head, London, for "Where Do You Sleep?" from *Lullabies and Night Songs* edited by William Engvick, copyright © 1965, Alec Wilder and William Engvick. Reprinted by permission of Harper & Row, Publishers, Inc. and The Bodley Head, London.

Houghton Mifflin/Clarion Books, for "I Want to Sleep," from *A Bunch of Poems and Verses* by Beatrice Shenk de Regniers, copyright © 1976, Beatrice Shenk de Regniers. Reprinted by permission of Houghton Mifflin/Clarion Books, New York.

William Kaufman, for "Catch Me the Moon, Daddy," by Griger Vitez, from *UNICEF Book of Children's Poems*, edited by William Kaufman. Reprinted by permission of William Kaufman.

J. B. Lippincott Company and Harold Ober Associates, Inc. for "The Night Will Never Stay," from *Eleanor Farjeon's Poems for Children* by Eleanor Farjeon, copyright © 1951, Eleanor Farjeon. Reprinted by permission of J. B. Lippincott Company and Harold Ober Associates, Inc.

Lothrop, Lee & Shepard Company, for "Lullaby," from *Everybody Has Two Eyes* by Jean Jaszi. Reprinted by permission of Lothrop, Lee & Shepard Company (a division of William Morrow & Company).

Macmillan Publishing Co., Inc., for "The Moon's the North Wind's Cooky," from *Collected Poems* by Vachel Lindsay, copyright 1914, Macmillan Publishing Co., Inc., renewed 1942, Elizabeth C. Lindsay. Reprinted by permission of Macmillan Publishing Co., Inc.

Eve Merriam, for "Lullaby," from *Out Loud* by Eve Merriam, copyright © 1973, Eve Merriam. Reprinted by permission of the author.

Marian Reiner, for "In Quiet Night," from *A Crazy Flight and Other Poems* by Myra Cohn Livingston, copyright © 1969, Myra Cohn Livingston; and "The Night," from *Whispers and Other Poems* by Myra Cohn Livingston, copyright © 1958, Myra Cohn Livingston; and "My Star," from *The Moon and A Star and Other Poems* by Myra Cohn Livingston, copyright © 1965, Myra Cohn Livingston. Reprinted by permission of Marian Reiner for the author.

Louise H. Sclove, for "Nocturne," from *The Light Guitar* and "The Starlighter," from *Gaily the Troubadour* by Arthur Guiterman. Reprinted by permission of Louise H. Sclove.

Charles Scribner's Sons, for "Bedtime," "Lullaby," and "Night Sounds," from *At the Top of My Voice* by Felice Holman, copyright © 1970, Felice Holman. Reprinted by permission of Charles Scribner's Sons.

Simon & Schuster, for "The Evening is Coming" and "Raindrops," from *The Fireside Book of Children's Songs*, edited by Marie Winn, copyright © 1966, Marie Winn and Allan Miller. Reprinted by permission of Simon & Schuster, a Division of Gulf & Western Corporation.

The United Educators, Inc., for "An East African Lullaby," translated by Holling C. Holling, from *The Book House for Children* by Olive Beaupre Miller. Reprinted by permission of The United Educators, Inc.

Contents

Bedtime Notes

Bedtime is a very special time for the young child. For the lucky one, it is a heartwarming time with the undivided attention of mother or father, even big sister or brother, reading, singing, and talking before the lights go off.

By the end of the day, most young children are exhausted physically and emotionally. They need a quiet period to unwind and restore the inner calm that leads to restful sleep. In the helter-skelter pattern of modern living, punctuated by the shrill voice of television, a child has little opportunity for the one-to-one communication that speaks personally. The bedtime hour can provide the warmth, the intimacy, the reinforcement so often missing in the day's activities.

When the Dark Comes Dancing is a collection of poems, lullabies, and lyrics which are bedtime favorites of young children and their parents.

Some of these are poems that grandmothers and grandfathers knew when they were children. Some are the creations of new poets. Several are the lyrics of old, old folk songs and lullabies from many lands and cultures. All have the freshness and simplicity which put them within the realm of even the youngest children.

In the right setting, they sing out to infants, toddlers, preschoolers, and kindergarteners and may remain their friends for years. Their appeal is all-embracing. An infant enjoys the melody of the lines and the full attention of an adult, half-singing, half-speaking to him or her alone. The toddler, who may have mastered only a few words and phrases, soon finds a way to echo lines from songs and poems. The preschooler and kindergartener may chime in on whole poems heard again and again, even improvising new lines to make the production a personal one.

11

If as an adult you have been a partner in a read-aloud period at bedtime, you will know the feeling of creating something with the child. You are doing it together, and together you rejoice.

This two-way satisfaction seems to grow more readily with planning:

- Before the child's bedtime hour, become acquainted with some of the poems and read them aloud so you can hear the effect of your own voice. Listen for ways to make it more pleasing, more musical. For the lullabies and folk songs, pull out the melody from your memory bank or from a song book and practice a bit. (A list of children's song books is given on page 73.)

- Any place where you are assured of peace and quiet is appropriate for bedtime poetry reading: at the child's bedside, in the living room, by the campfire on vacation—wherever you and the child can be so close as to feel the warm presence of each other and drift into a peaceful mood.

- A fixed time each evening makes the child feel this is important to you as well as to him or her, and the positive effect increases.

- Let there be no interruptions. No hectic demands of others in the household. No guests dropping in. No telephone calls. No TV programs to distract you. The bedtime poetry hour should be apart from all of that.

- Whether the child is tucked into bed or sitting on your lap, hold the book so that pictures can be enjoyed. Even a six-month-old baby learns to look at the pages.

- Begin with a poem or song the child knows, perhaps one that he or she chooses. Then move to one that ties into something current in the child's experience. If it is raining, you may want to try the old Slovak lullaby, "Raindrops." If you had a bedtime look at the stars, try "By'm Bye" and "My Star." After listening to the outdoor sounds at bedtime, read "Night Sounds." The poems you read and the songs you sing will depend on the mood that develops each evening between you and the child.

- While it is important to plunge in and keep going, be sure to take time for repetition and the child's response. Often a young child needs to hear something several times before being sure what response is right for him or her.

- As a child becomes more at home with poetry and song, he or she may enjoy helping you with reading and singing. This kind of involvement comes gradually. The old Texas folk song "By'm Bye" makes a lovely starter because it has so many "by'm byes" to be sung again and again. Four- and five-year-olds will enjoy echoing the dream fantasy of Beatrice Schenk de Regniers: "of elephants flying" and "of cantaloupes crying." Then they will chime in on her series beginning "a million, a billion, a trillion" and gloat over mastery of such words.

- Sometimes it is fun to adapt a poem or song to include the name of the child or his pets and friends. "Hush, little baby, don't say a word" can be easily converted to "Listen, my Stevie, don't say a word," for a more grown-up listener.
- Singing will add to the magic of the bedtime hour. For this reason several of the familiar lullabies are included. Soon you will find that some of the poems seem to sing out their own melody, and you can easily chant them or half-sing them in your own way. I find myself singing "The Stars, the Dark, and the Daisies" to the tune of "The Bear Went Over the Mountain." That was certainly not the poet's intent, but I think she wouldn't mind.

After all, the purpose of the bedtime poetry hour is to bring the child's day to a close with shared pleasure in simple beauty and loveliness.

> *Stars are shining*
> *Children singing*
> *By'm, by'm bye.*
> *Children nodding*
> *Children sleeping*
> *By'm bye . . .*

—Nancy Larrick

Little Creatures Everywhere Are Settling Down to Sleep

For the young child, bedtime means separation from the rest of the family and the hubbub of family life. The later the hour the more weary the child becomes, and the more he or she may protest going to bed. The prospect of poetry and song can make bedtime a period to look forward to and to cherish.

It is reassuring to the child to remember that evening is the time when many creatures go to sleep—the crow, the pony, the donkey, the sheep, the pig, the old black cat, the turtle, the honeybee . . .

Little creatures everywhere
Are settling down to sleep.

Hushabye My Darling

Hushabye my darling
Don't you make a peep
Little creatures everywhere
Are settling down to sleep

Fishes in the millpond
Goslings in the barn
Kitten by the fireside
Baby in my arms

Listen to the raindrops
Singing you to sleep
Hushabye my darling
Don't you make a peep

Clyde Watson

17

Little Donkey Close Your Eyes

Little Donkey on the hill
Standing there so very still
Making faces at the skies
Little Donkey close your eyes.

Little Monkey in the tree
Swinging there so merrily
Throwing cocoanuts at the skies
Little Monkey close your eyes.

Silly Sheep that slowly crop
Night has come and you must stop
Chewing grass beneath the skies
Little Sheep now close your eyes.

Little Pig that squeals about
Make no noises with your snout

No more squealing to the skies
Little Pig now close your eyes.

Wild young birds that sweetly sing
Curve your heads beneath your wing
Dark night covers all the skies
Wild young birds now close your eyes.

Old black cat down in the barn
Keeping five small kittens warm
Let the wind blow in the skies
Dear old black cat close your eyes.

Little child all tucked in bed
Looking such a sleepy head
Stars are quiet in the skies
Little child now close your eyes.

Margaret Wise Brown

19

The Evening Is Coming

(A SONG)

The evening is coming, the sun sinks to rest,
The birds are all flying straight home to their nests,
''Caw, caw,'' says the crow as he flies overhead,
It's time little children were going to bed.

Here comes the pony, his work is all done,
Down through the meadow he takes a good run,
Up go his heels—and down goes his head.
It's time little children were going to bed.

Author Unknown

Bedtime

Now the mouse goes to his hole,
In ribboned coils the small snakes roll,
Down at the stream, the tired tadpole,
    Atop the oak, the oriole.

Bowed heads on every sleeping squill,
The tender tulip, daffodil,
Anemones all stand quite still,
    And in the woods, the whippoorwill.

Back to his hive, the honeybee,
The turtle to his armory,
And I to bed go sleepily,
    And in the tree, the chickadee.

                Felice Holman

Where Do You Sleep?

(A SONG)

The green worm sleeps in silk
The turtle sleeps in sand
And the bluebird sleeps in a feather bed
The yak prefers to stand
The white lamb sleeps in wool
The ermine sleeps in fur
But the monkey sleeps in his mommy's arms
All warm and close to her.

William Engvik

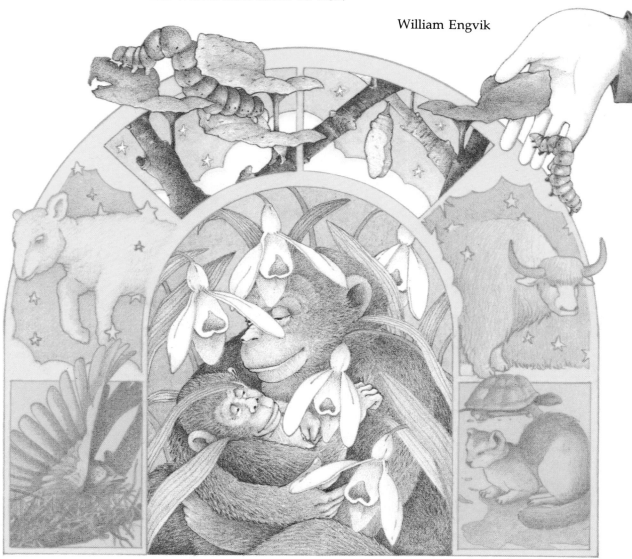

Storm at Night

When I'm tucked in bed,
Comfortable and warm,
I often think of animals
        Outside in the storm:

The deer in hemlock thickets,
(A little out of the rain),
A wet fox going on his rounds
        For supper once again;

Hungry hares in their burrows;
A flood in the woodchuck's hole;
Chipmunks cuddled together;
        A half-drowned, star-nosed mole.

I lie in my bed and shiver
And think of what Father said,
''If you were a creature of the woods,
You wouldn't like house and bed!''

Elizabeth Coatsworth

23

The Stars Danced
Over the Daisies

There is no more beautiful way to get ready for bed than to have one last, lingering look at the moon and the stars. If you live in the country, you are blessed, for just one sweeping look from your doorstep on a clear night is awe-inspiring. Even the very young enjoy noting the stars in all directions. They like to talk about the great round full moon or the tiny sliver of a new moon.

If you live in the city, you may see only a piece of sky from your window with just a star or two. But when you are in the park some evening—away from the glare of streetlights and billboards—you can enjoy the wider vista and help the child find more stars and possibly the moon as well.

Then at your bedside poetry hour read some of the poems and sing some of the songs that tell of the moon and the stars at bedtime.

The Stars, the Dark, and the Daisies

The Dark danced over the daisies,
the daisies, the daisies,
the Dark danced over the daisies,
and all the daisies hid—
they tucked their heads in the clover—
the Dark went dancing over—
they tucked their heads in the clover
      and hid away, they did!

The Stars danced over the daisies,
the daisies, the daisies,
the Stars danced over the daisies,
and oh, they were so bright,
the daisies went a'dancing,
in Starlight went a'dancing,
until their pretty meadow
was full of a lovely light . . .

         Ivy O. Eastwick

27

Lullaby

The moon and the stars and the wind in the sky
All night long sing a lullaby,
While down in the ocean so dark and so deep
The silvery waves rock the fishes to sleep.

Jean Jaszi

My Star

My star comes out
When I'm in bed,
    There is a place to put my head
    where I can watch it twinkle
    high
    in one small windowpane of sky.

Myra Cohn Livingston

The Starlighter

When the bat's on the wing and the bird's in the tree,
Comes the old starlighter whom none may see.
First in the west, where the low hills are,
He touches the wand to the evening star.
Then swiftly he runs on his rounds on high
Till he's lit ev'ry lamp in the dark blue sky.

Arthur Guiterman

29

By'm Bye

(TEXAS FOLK SONG)

By'm bye,
By'm bye.
Stars shining.
Number, number one,
number two, number three,
Good Lawd, by'm bye, by'm bye.
Good Lawd, by'm bye.

Traditional

The Moon's the North Wind's Cooky

(WHAT THE LITTLE GIRL SAID)

The Moon's the North Wind's cooky.
He bites it, day by day,
Until there's but a rim of scraps
That crumble all away.

The South Wind is a baker.
He kneads clouds in his den,
And bakes a crisp new moon *that . . . greedy*
North . . . Wind . . . eats . . . again!

Vachel Lindsay

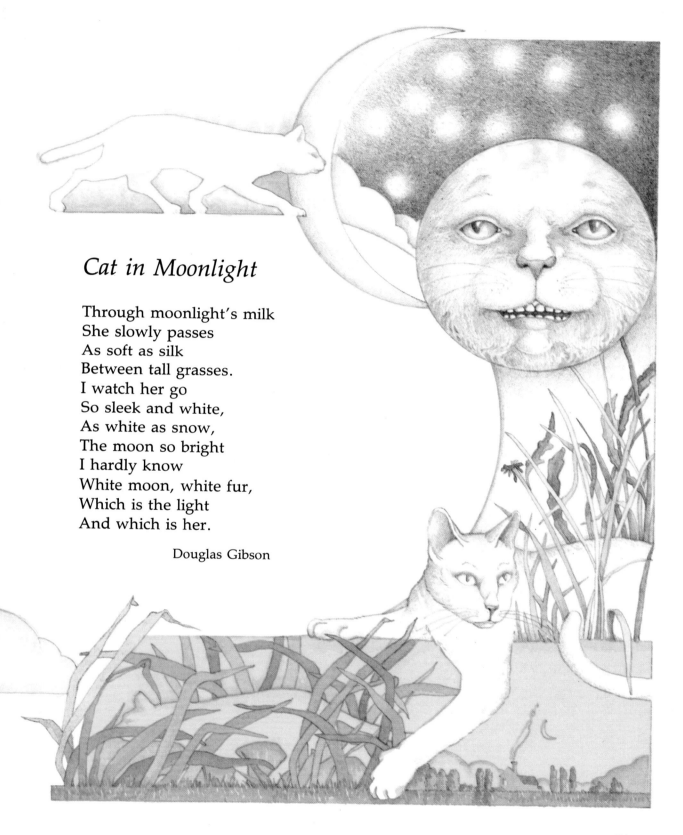

Cat in Moonlight

Through moonlight's milk
She slowly passes
As soft as silk
Between tall grasses.
I watch her go
So sleek and white,
As white as snow,
The moon so bright
I hardly know
White moon, white fur,
Which is the light
And which is her.

Douglas Gibson

31

Until We Built a Cabin

When we lived in a city
(three flights up and down)
I never dreamed how many stars
could show above a town.

When we moved to a village
where lighted streets were few,
I thought I could see all the stars,
But, oh, I never knew—

Until we built a cabin
where hills are high and far,
I never knew how many
                many
                        stars there really are!

Aileen Fisher

Last Song

To the Sun
Who has shone
    All day,
To the Moon
Who has gone
    Away,
To the milk-white,
Silk-white,
Lily-white Star
A fond goodnight
Wherever you are.

James Guthrie

33

There's Nothing Sweeter than The Middle of the Night

What do we hear when the lights are turned off at night? Street sounds—
"Wheels humming/heels drumming"? Or "the tipping, tapping, rapping/In the middle of the wall"?

Take a few minutes to note the night sounds with your child and talk about them. If you help identify the after-dark sounds, he or she is less likely to be fearful of being alone in the dark.

Then read some of the poems that tell of the night sounds—even the night pictures—that make bedtime a very special time.

The Middle of the Night

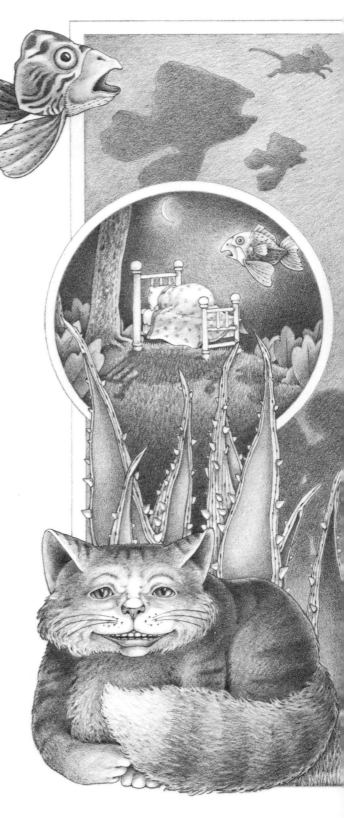

This is a song to be sung at night
When nothing is left of you and the light
When the cats don't bark
And the mice don't moo
And the nightmares come and nuzzle you
When there's blackness in the cupboards
And the closet and the hall
And a tipping, tapping, rapping
In the middle of the wall
When the lights have one by one gone out
All over everywhere
And a shadow by the curtains
Bumps a shadow by the chair
Then you hide beneath your pillow
With your eyes shut very tight
And you sing
''There's nothing sweeter than
The middle of the night.
I'm extremely fond of shadows
And I really must confess
That cats and bats don't scare me
Well, they couldn't scare me less
And most of all I like the things
That slide and slip and creep.''
It really is surprising
How fast you fall asleep.

Karla Kuskin

Nocturne

The three-toed tree toad
Sings his sweet ode
     To the moon:
The funny bunny
And his honey
     trip in tune.
The gentle cricket
From his thicket
     Lifts his croon;
A love-lorn owlet
Of his fowlet
     Begs a boon.
Across the water
To her daughter
     Calls the loon;
A happy froglet
From his boglet
     Chants a rune.
The yellow hound-dog
And the brown dog
     Bay the 'coon;
The chipmunk dozes
Where the rose's
     Leaves are strewn;
All through the night-time
Till the bright time
     Comes, too soon,
The three-toed tree toad
Sings his sweet ode
     To the moon.

Arthur Guiterman

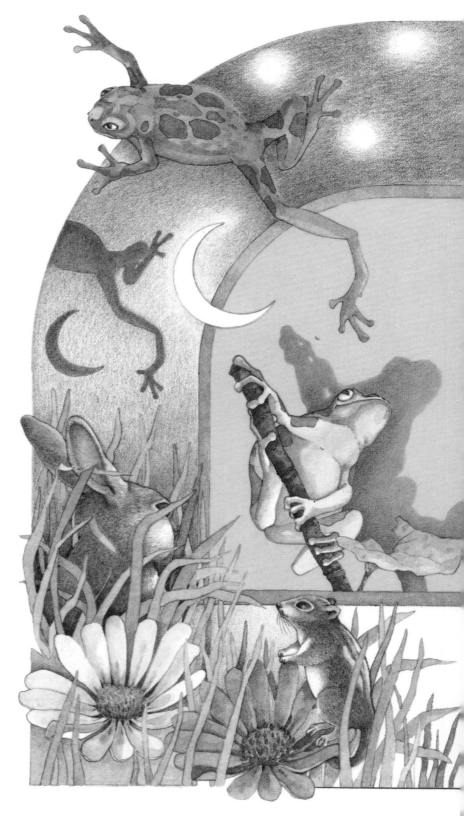

38

The Night Will Never Stay

The night will never stay,
The night will still go by,
Though with a million stars
You pin it to the sky;
Though you bind it with the blowing wind
And buckle it with the moon,
The night will slip away
Like a sorrow or a tune.

Eleanor Farjeon

39

Night Sounds

In the street
      sounds of wheels humming,
      sounds of heels drumming.
Humming and drumming,
Keeping me from sleeping.
In the house
      sounds of words mumbling,
      overheard grumbling.
Mumbling and grumbling,
Keeping me unsleeping.
Far away
      sounds of waves lashing,
      quietly crashing.
Lashing and crashing,
Sweeping me to sleep.

Felice Holman

In Quiet Night

In quiet night
the horns honking up from the street
make mad voices
to other horns, tires shriek
to other tires, brakes shriek
to other brakes.

Somewhere, there is a night of trees,
of great, bulging bullfrogs croaking
in ponds. Screech owls cry to a forest
of birds
      shrieking.

Horns, in quiet night, honk up songs
no frog, no bird, has ever sung.

          Myra Cohn Livingston

The Train in the Night

Who hears in the night
The train's sharp whistle
Cut off the top
Of chickweed and thistle
Flutter the birds
That drowse in the willow
And rouse the boy
From his frosty pillow?

Who hears in the night
The wheels that mutter
Past mill and grave
Past barn and shutter
Is the boy for whom
All time unravels
Who'll swallow the wind
And go on his travels.

Elizabeth Riddell

Windy Nights

Whenever the moon and stars are set,
    Whenever the wind is high,
All night long in the dark and wet,
    A man goes riding by.
Late in the night when the fires are out,
Why does he gallop and gallop about?

Whenever the trees are crying aloud,
    And ships are tossed at sea,
By, on the highway, low and loud
    By at the gallop goes he.
By at the gallop goes he, and then
By he comes back at the gallop again.

               Robert Louis Stevenson

Sleeping Outdoors

Under the dark is a star,
Under the star is a tree,
Under the tree is a blanket,
And under the blanket is me.

Marchette Chute

The Night

The night
    creeps in
    around my head
    and snuggles down
    upon the bed,
    and makes lace pictures
    on the wall
    but doesn't say a word at all.

Myra Cohn Livingston

Lullaby

The trees now look scary.
It's dusk and we're wary
    of hedges and sedges
    that border the edges
    of birches and larches
    and beeches in arches
    of maples and apples
    and shadows in dapples.
The willows are weeping
It's time we were sleeping.

Felice Holman

Now the Day Is Over
(A SONG)

Now the day is over
    Night is drawing nigh,
Shadows of the evening
    Steal across the sky.

Now the darkness gathers,
    Stars begin to peep
Birds, and beasts, and flowers
    Soon will be asleep.

Sabine Baring-Gould

Winter Night

As I lie in bed I hear
The east wind crying in my ear,
And soon will follow, soft and low,
The sifting whisper of the snow.

Marchette Chute

47

The Moon Will Weave Sweet Dreams

Often bedtime leads to dreamtime, which is fascinating to a child.
Where do dreams come from? Where do they go? What will I dream about? Such questions can spur a child's imagination and lead easily to the children's poems about dreams and the loving good-night:

Happy dreams & sleep tight.

Catch Me the Moon, Daddy

Catch me the moon, Daddy,
Let it shine near me for a while,
Catch me the moon, Daddy,
I want to touch its smile.

The moon must shine from high above;
That's where it needs to stay
Among the stars, to guide them home
When they return from play.

So the bunny can find his supper,
So the mouse can scamper free,
So the hedgehog can make his forays,
So the birds can sleep in the tree.

And as for you, my child,
With slender silver thread
The moon will weave sweet dreams, so you
May slumber in your bed.

Griger Vitez

All Tucked in & Roasty Toasty

All tucked in & roasty toasty
Blow me a kiss good-night
Close your eyes till morning comes
Happy dreams & sleep tight

Clyde Watson

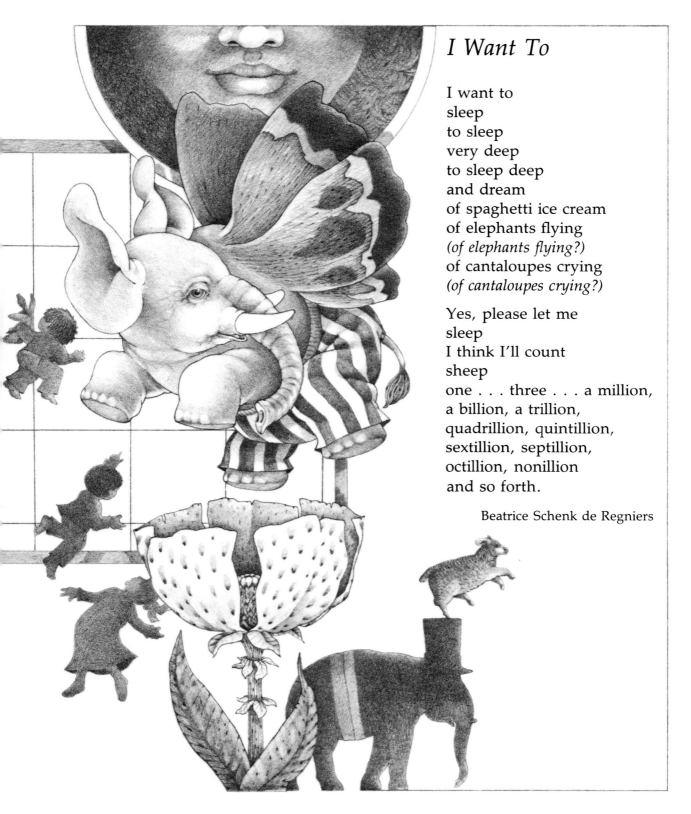

I Want To

I want to
sleep
to sleep
very deep
to sleep deep
and dream
of spaghetti ice cream
of elephants flying
(of elephants flying?)
of cantaloupes crying
(of cantaloupes crying?)

Yes, please let me
sleep
I think I'll count
sheep
one . . . three . . . a million,
a billion, a trillion,
quadrillion, quintillion,
sextillion, septillion,
octillion, nonillion
and so forth.

Beatrice Schenk de Regniers

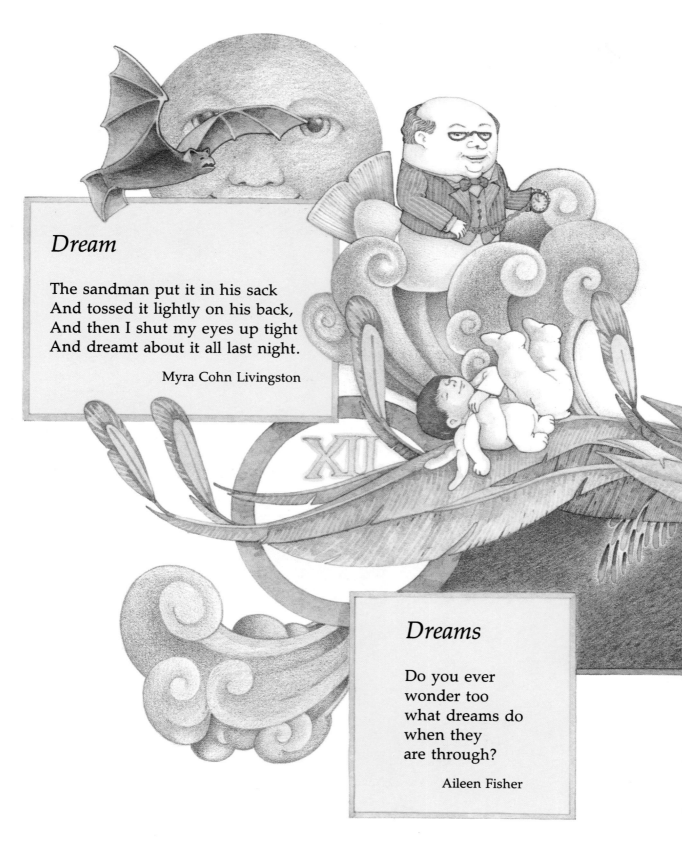

Dream

The sandman put it in his sack
And tossed it lightly on his back,
And then I shut my eyes up tight
And dreamt about it all last night.

Myra Cohn Livingston

Dreams

Do you ever
wonder too
what dreams do
when they
are through?

Aileen Fisher

Sleep, Baby, Sleep
(GERMAN LULLABY)

Sleep, baby, sleep!
Thy father watches the sheep;
Thy mother is shaking the dreamland tree,
And down falls a little dream on thee:
Sleep, baby, sleep!

Sleep, baby, sleep!
The large stars are the sheep;
The wee stars are the lambs, I guess,
The fair moon is the shepherdess:
Sleep, baby, sleep!

Traditional

55

Singing You Their Lullabies

In every part of the world people sing lullabies to their children at bedtime. Many of these are old songs which reflect the way of life of those who sing them or of the land in which they live. A Nigerian lullaby tells of drums beating on the River Benue. An East African song notes that rain is bending the sugar cane. And a lullaby from the Canadian Province of New Brunswick tells of the baby's cradle swinging by an old rocking chair.

Old lullabies and new are soothing and reassuring. Sing the old melodies if you know them. Or create your own rhythm—reading softly, gently, half-crooning, half-chanting . . .

Sleep, my baby, sleep.

Raindrops

(SLOVAK LULLABY)

Raindrops a-falling from the skies,
Tired and sleepy, close your eyes.
Tired and sleepy
While the skies are weeping,
Weeping and singing you their lullabies.
Tired and sleepy,
While the skies are weeping,
Weeping and singing you their lullabies.

Traditional

Benue Lullaby

(MODERN AFRICAN LULLABY)

The River Benue (rhymes with *Janeway*) is in Nigeria.

The fishing boats sway
On the Benue
Under a fingernail moon so white
Under a fingernail moon so white

Bullfrogs croak in Benue
And the moon is a sliver of light so bright
And the moon is a sliver of light so bright

Drums are beating in Benue
Beat booming through the night
And fireflies dance in Benue
In flashes of silvery white
In flashes of silvery white

Beat boom the drums in Benue
Beat boom the drums through the night
Shine crescent moon on Benue
Fingernail sliver of light
Fingernail sliver of light

Dance fireflies in Benue
In flashes of silvery white
And sleep little ones in Benue
Sleep on sleep on through the night
Sleep on sleep on through the night

Martin Brennan

Sleep, Sleep, My Little One
(EAST AFRICAN LULLABY)

Sleep, sleep, my little one! The night is all wind and rain;
The meal has been wet by the raindrops
        and bent is the sugar cane;
O Giver who gives to the people, in safety my little son keep!
My little son with the headdress, sleep, sleep, sleep!

Traditional
(Translated by Holling C. Holling)

Rockabye Baby
(CANADIAN LULLABY)

Rockabye baby, so sweet and so fair
While mother sits by in her old rocking chair,
With her foot on the rocker the cradle she swings,
And though baby slumbers he hears what she sings.

Rockabye baby on the treetop
When the wind blows the cradle will rock
When the bough breaks the cradle will fall.
Down will come baby and cradle and all.

Rockabye, rockabye, nothing to fear
Rockabye, rockabye, mother is near;
With her foot on the rocker the cradle she swings,
And though baby slumbers he hears what she sings.

Traditional

Lullaby
(ENGLISH LULLABY)

Flowers are closed and lambs are sleeping;
Lullaby, oh, lullaby!
Stars are up, the moon is peeping;
Lullaby, oh, lullaby!

While the birds are silence keeping,
Lullaby, oh, lullaby!
Sleep, my baby, fall a-sleeping,
Lullaby, oh, lullaby!

Christina Rossetti

Hush, Little Baby

Hush, little baby, don't say a word,
Mama's going to buy you a mocking bird.

And if that mocking bird don't sing,
Mama's going to buy you a diamond ring.

And if that diamond ring turns to brass,
Mama's going to buy you a looking glass.

And if that looking glass gets broke,
Mama's going to buy you a billy goat.

And if that billy goat won't pull,
Mama's going to buy you a cart and bull.

And if that cart and bull turn over,
Mama's going to buy you a dog named Rover.

And if that dog named Rover won't bark,
Mama's going to buy you a horse and cart.

And if that horse and cart fall down
You'll still be the sweetest little baby in town.

Traditional

65

Hush 'n' Bye

(SOUTH CAROLINA FOLK SONG)

Hush 'n' Bye, don't you cry
Oh, you pretty little baby,
When you wake you'll have some cake
And all the pretty little ponies,
A brown and a gray and a black and a bay,
And all the pretty little ponies.

Traditional

66

Rock, Rock, Sleep, My Baby

Rock, rock, sleep, my baby
Sings the sweet cuckoo . . .
When your Daddy comes back home
He'll bring a toy for you.

Hush, hush, sleep, my baby
Sleep the whole night through . . .
When your Daddy comes back home
He'll sing a song for you.

Clyde Watson

Lullaby
(AFRICAN LULLABY)

Someone would like to have you for her child
but you are mine.
Someone would like to rear you on a costly mat
but you are mine.
Someone would like to place you on a camel blanket
but you are mine.
I have you to rear on a torn old mat.
Someone would like to have you as her child
but you are mine.

Traditional

68

Kentucky Babe

(LULLABY)

Skeeters are a-humming on the honeysuckle vine,
Sleep, Kentucky Babe!
Sandman is a-coming to this little babe of mine,
Sleep, Kentucky Babe!
Silvery moon is shining in the heavens up above,
Bobolink is pining for his little lady love,
You are mighty lucky,
Babe of old Kentucky,
Close your eyes in sleep.
> *Fly away,*
> *Fly away, Kentucky Babe, fly away to rest,*
> *Fly away,*
> *Lay your tiny curly head on your mommy's breast*
> *Hm . . . Hm . . .*
> *Close your eyes in sleep.*

Author Unknown

Lullaby

Sh   sh   what do you wish
sh   sh   the windows are shuttered
sh   sh   a magical fish
swims out from the window and down to the river

lap   lap   the waters are lapping
sh   sh   the shore slips away
glide   glide   glide   with the current
sh   sh   the shadows are deeper

sleep   sleep   tomorrow is sure

Eve Merriam

71

Sleep Now and Rest
(RUSSIAN LULLABY)

Sleep, my baby, sleep now and rest,
Safe as a fledgling in its wee nest.
Sleep now and rest, safe in your nest.
Sleep, my baby, sleep.

Traditional

Books of Poems and Songs for Children

Songs for the Very Young

American Folk Songs for Children. Edited by Ruth Crawford Seeger. Doubleday.
The Baby's Song Book. Edited by Elizabeth Poston. Crowell.
The Fireside Book of Children's Songs. Edited by Marie Winn and Allan Miller.
  Simon and Schuster.
The Fireside Book of Folk Songs. Edited by Margaret Bradford Boni.
  Simon and Schuster.
Lullabies and Night Songs. Edited by William Engvick. Harper.
Mister Rogers' Songbook by Fred Rogers. Random.
Rockabye Baby: Lullabies from Many Nations and Peoples. Compiled by Carl S. Miller.
  Published in cooperation with UNICEF. Chappell Music Co.
Sing Mother Goose. Illus. by Marjorie Torrey. Dutton.
Sing Together Children. Edited by Frances M. Andrews. Cooperative Recreation
  Services, Inc. Radnor Rd. Delaware, Ohio 43015.

Nursery Rhymes and Mother Goose

Brian Wildsmith's Mother Goose (Selections from). Scholastic.
Hi Diddle Diddle, A Book of Mother Goose. Scholastic.
Mother Goose. Illus. by Gyo Fujikawa. Grosset.
The Mother Goose Treasury. Illus. by Raymond Briggs. Coward.
The Puffin Book of Mother Goose. Compiled by Iona and Peter Opie. Penguin.
The Tall Book of Mother Goose. Illus. by Feodor Rojankovsky. Harper.

Poetry for the Very Young

Catch Me & Kiss Me & Say It Again. Clyde Watson. Philomel.
Father Fox's Pennyrhymes. Clyde Watson. Crowell.
Hello and Good-By. Mary Ann Hoberman. Little, Brown.
I Went to the Animal Fair. Edited by William Cole. Philomel.
More Poems to Read to the Very Young. Edited by Josette Frank. Random.
Nibble Nibble. Margaret Wise Brown. Addison-Wesley.
Poems and Verses to Begin On. Edited by Donald J. Bissett. Chandler.
Poems Children Will Sit Still For. Edited by Beatrice de Regniers et al. Scholastic.

Poems for Galloping, Poems for Counting, and *Poems for Weather Watching.* Edited by Bill Martin, Jr. (Little Owl Books) Holt.

Poems to Read to the Very Young. Edited by Josette Frank. Random.

Roar and More. Karla Kushkin. Harper.

Sun Through Small Leaves: Poems of Spring. Edited by Satomi Ichikawa. Philomel.

Under the Cherry Tree. Edited by Cynthia Mitchell. Philomel.

Where Have You Been? Margaret Wise Brown. Scholastic.

Whispers and Other Poems. Myra Cohn Livingston. Harcourt.

Index of First Lines

Index of Poets, Poems and Songs

About the Author

Nancy Larrick is a distinguished educator and the editor of many anthologies of poetry for young readers, including *On City Streets, Piping Down the Valleys Wild, Room for Me and a Mountain Lion,* and, most recently, *Bring Me All of Your Dreams* She is also widely known as the author of *A Parent's Guide to Children's Reading,* which was a direct outgrowth of her doctoral dissertation at New York University and won the Edison Foundation Award as an outstanding contribution to education. Nancy Larrick grew up in Winchester, Virginia, where she now lives.

About the Artist

John Wallner received his BFA from Washington University in St. Louis and his Master's degree from Pratt Institute of Art. His picture books have won many awards, including the AIGA Certificate of Excellence, and he has designed a bookmark and a streamer for the Children's Book Council. He and his wife, who is also an artist, live in Woodstock, New York.